White Apocalypse

New England's Blizzard of `78 and its three day rampage of death and destruction by land and by sea...

Alan R. Earls

DEDICATION

Dedicated to the memory of those lost in the Blizzard of `78.

CONTENTS

ACKNOWLEDGMENTS

This book would not have been possible without the help of those who generously made available photos of the Blizzard of `78. Photos are marked with the names of sources throughout.

1 SURPRISE ATTACK

Monday, Feb. 6, 1978, was a rather typical New England winter morning with temperatures in the teens or twenties and a gray, cloudy sky. Some particularly weather-wise individuals may have expected a major storm, with the first flakes of snow before 8 am, and a few took steps to prepare. But, in part because few meteorologists spotted the threat, most of New England went on its merry way, largely oblivious to what was in store. Not until late morning or even early afternoon of the 6th did the storm begin to attract notice. Indicators changed rapidly, with a rising wind from the north and winds that ranged from 20-40 mph in the afternoon. By then, snow was accumulating at the rate of an inch per hour or more.

It looked big. Big enough for some people to head home early, big enough for some schools to close at mid-day, and big enough for the media to finally take notice.

But these were hardy times. Employers ran to time clocks and rigid schedules and time off for weather emergencies was highly unusual. So, although some were able to avoid a confrontation with the storm, almost everyone else just waited and assumed, as New Englanders, there wasn't much that Mother Nature could do that hadn't already been done.

When the trickle of homeward bound people – many already discovering just how hard getting home could be – turned into a regular evening rush hour, chaos followed. The one saving grace was perhaps the fact that Boston area highways were probably at their most commodious relative to the volume of traffic they needed to handle. Every major current day highway was in place – minus some of the later improvements such as the "Big Dig" that depressed Boston's Central Artery. So, somehow, commuters usually got where they needed to go without too many slowdowns. But there were, of course, exceptions, especially when snow fell. Most cars lacked the traction benefits of front-wheel drive or all-wheel drive and sometimes couldn't quite navigate exit ramps or steeper inclines. Years of bleak economic times had put others on a tight budget, so snow tires were a luxury item that not everyone could afford. Thus, traffic slowed on that Monday afternoon. This day, snow accumulated and, in short order, hundreds, and then thousands of cars and their drivers and passengers found themselves immobilized. And any hope plow drivers had of keeping the road opened quickly faded as the wind howled and drivers came to realize their very survival was now in jeopardy.

But their problems were nothing compared to the crisis facing areas along the shore. To the challenge of ever deepening, heavy snow was added the dread team of wind and water, the later emboldened by coincident astronomical high tides -- even the moon was conspiring against the region – brought record high tides, flooding, and pounding surf.

Among those able to leave "early" was Douglas Wynne, at the time a resident of Norwood, Mass. He had started his work day in Saugus. Calling his wife at mid-day, he heard from her that the storm was having a big impact south of the city and in Rhode Island. Reluctantly, he decided to head toward home via Route 1 and the Mystic River Bridge. So far so good. And even the often-temperamental Southeast Expressway seemed to be moving okay, until his car crossed the Neponset River Bridge. There, traffic stopped and there were still many miles yet to go. A native of Dorchester; he knew the region's secondary roads. So, at his first opportunity, he exited the highway and looked for the avenue of least resistance that would lead to Norwood. That path of opportunity eventually led to Sharon and a hood-height drift across the road that his compact Mercury Comet was not about to challenge. Several alternate routes and a total of five and a half hours after departing Saugus, he finally managed to ram his tired car into his snow-filled driveway.

Around that time the author was reporting for "second shift" at computer data center in Cambridge, Mass. It had been a short drive from a friend's place in Allston, Mass. Snowy and a bit slow but just another day in New England. The weather was part of the day's small talk but feeding the printers and performing the usual variety of software checks on the Amdahl 470 garnered more attention.

So, it was with tremendous surprise that the three or four team members on duty learned from their boss just before 7 p.m. – as they contemplated a supper break – that they were being sent home. What's more, one of the day staff who had stayed late had decided to book a hotel nearby for the night because he had heard the roads had become impassable.

Leaving the company parking garage a little later and bound for suburban Wayland, the scene was surreal. Side streets were rutted and often not plowed at all. Main roads had clearly been plowed at some point but often still had several inches of recent snow. Most surprising of all was the traffic or lack of it. There were cars on the road but all of them were parked and buried under at least a foot of snow. At no point in the next 90 minutes of low-gear, pedal-to-the-metal driving did I see a single passenger car driving – just one or two plows.

And whether I would make it was in doubt. The modest hill that takes state Route 30 into Weston, Mass. required careful driving as the rear-wheels constantly threatened to "fishtail" on the slippery surface, with the deep snow crunching continually beneath the floorboards.

Upon reaching my parent's home in Wayland I was confronted with a wall of snow at least three feet high – and an unplowed driveway with nearly as much snow within. So, I drove on another half-mile and, like several other people facing a similar predicament, abandoned my vehicle in the Brockleman's grocery store parking lot.

Then, and only then did the real fury of the storm become apparent. Bitter wind and driving snow stood between me and my family's front door. I was blessed with a down jacket and thanked heavens I was young and reasonably fit. Every forward movement was exhausting. And then, just before reaching my own home, out of the storm emerged a younger neighbor – Ernest DiMuzio -- running a snow blower back and forth and trying to keep the storm at bay; at least for his parent's driveway. Although normal for any other storm, his sudden appearance before me in this freezing, flesh jabbing maelstrom and our brief exchange of pleasantries seemed like a miracle.

While I was able to make it to my destination, at that point in the storm, most others simply had to stay put.

A work colleague of the author's in the 1990s, Leslie Scott-Lysan, at the time was heavily involved with WBIM, the student-run radio station at Bridgewater State College. The blizzard had isolated the studio so that only she and one other staffer were able to make it there for the first few days of the storm. What's more WBIM was a participant in the emergency broadcast system and was expected to be ready to broadcast emergency messages from government authorities. Although the system was aimed primarily at communications in the event of a nuclear attack, the Blizzard – already being spoken of as the storm of the century – also qualified as an emergency. So, Scott-Lysan and her colleague racked their brains for things to talk about and kept broadcasting non-stop, with only a few brief moments of the dread "dead air" until relief finally arrived.

The storm itself was a combination of three weather systems combined into an on-shore storm known at the time as a northeaster (subsequently corrupted to nor'easter in common usage). One storm was born over the Atlantic, another came up the coast from the southeastern part of the US and a third formed originally over western Pennsylvania. The final ingredient was a strong high pressure over eastern Canada that held the forces in place. What developed was a cyclonic pattern of onshore winds laden with moisture in the form of show. Sustained winds were often above 60 miles per hour and gusts went much higher. Up to four inches of snow per hour fell on some spots and with the strong winds, drifts up to 15 feet deep formed in many locations – nearly burying some houses and many cars.

Although Eastern Massachusetts and Rhode Island bore the brunt of the storm, its effects were felt in Connecticut, as far west as New York and New Jersey and to the north into Maine and New Hampshire. Dr. Jeffrey Lamont, a Boston-area urologist, recalled that Dartmouth College, where he was an undergraduate in 1978, actually shut down – a highly unusual event for the campus.

Geography made the storm especially dangerous within Massachusetts Bay, where fearsome winds and tide were trapped. According to Massachusetts officials, the ocean rose as much as 15.2 feet above mean low water. But individual waves were often much higher and the persistent wind drove water far inland. Severe erosion was also a consequence of the wind and waves. In addition to demolishing concrete walls and roadways in areas such as Nantasket Beach (Hull) and Revere beach, the Pamet River, really more of an ocean inlet, located near the tip of Cape Cod, was turned into a passage all the way across the peninsula by the storm, effectively turning the area around Provincetown into an island.

Two individuals came to symbolize the storm – both governors. Recently elected Massachusetts Democrat, Michael Stanley Dukakis helmed the Bay State's response and J. Joseph Garrahy, his Democrat opposite number in Rhode Island. And both become iconic thanks to their wardrobe choice. Dukakis put aside his suit and tie and spoke to the people in person and through live broadcasts often wearing a cardigan sweater reminiscent of the one that made children's television "star" Fred Rogers ("Mr. Rogers") famous. And, across the border in Rhode Island, Garrahy faced the storm in a signature plaid flannel shirt.

2 (STRANDED) TRAINS, PLANES, AND AUTOMOBILES

By the numbers, the storm was impressive, hundreds of drivers were trapped in cars that couldn't drive any further, particularly along Route 128. The grim choice was between risking a long and dangerous walk to safety, staying in the car and freezing, or running the car and risking carbon monoxide poisoning. The Dedham Cinema, located adjacent to the Route 1 interchange, became a de facto shelter for dozens of people.

Less obvious to the average person in the storm than the impassible roads was the impact on other modes of transportation. Trains of every variety struggled through the storm and then eventually, stopped.

Several years ago, Marcelle Enright, sharing recollections with the Milford Daily News, recalled the experiences of Jimmy Enright, who had started working for the railroad in the region in 1934, when it was known and the Boston & Albany. Three name changes later – it was Conrail in 1978 – Enright was astonished to find that for the first time in his career, a snowstorm had shut down operations.

The family lived on Cross Street in Bellingham and Marcelle recalled hand-shoveling the driveway, all 200 feet of it, in the morning so Jimmy could drive to work. But when Jimmy finally got to Framingham he found no yardmaster to supervise operations – in fact no one at all! After ending up in snowdrifts a few times in his full-size Ford LTD wagon, Jimmy finally made it back home. But there was to be no respite. As soon as the snow ended, it was back to work for real: trains needed to get back in operation and railroad workers were thus freed from the prohibition on driving. And that put Jimmy and his car in demand from neighbors who begged him to pick up basic food and other items on his route to and from work.

1978, the year of a town bicentennial in Franklin Massachusetts, was also the year that nature dumped a record 54 inches of snow during the Blizzard of '78. Teacher Robert Vallee kept measuring snow levels throughout the storm, and reporting them to Boston TV channels—it turned out that Franklin had some of the heaviest snow of any place in Massachusetts. That had meant closing school early on the first day of the storm. But this simply meant sending children into the snow to walk home on their own or discharging students at their regular bus stops. Vicki Buchanio, at the time an 11-year-old in Franklin, recalled searching for her two younger sisters who had opted to walk the half-mile from the Davis Thayer School. Eventually, with the help of her father, John Buchanio, Vicki found her sisters struggling across the town common. The endings of such stories were not always happy. Not far away, in Uxbridge, 10-year-old Peter Gosselin, disappeared on Feb. 7 and was found weeks later just feet from his home, buried in a deep snowbank.

Meanwhile, in Franklin that day, Howard Crawford and other DPW workers went to work from the start to clear roads paralyzed by snow. Driving a dump truck down Oak Street at nightfall, Crawford found himself following a four-wheel drive vehicle. The car in front of him slammed on its brakes, coming to a stop, and then started up again going through the snow with relative ease; but Crawford's truck, with two-wheel drive, stalled in the snow. He had to spend the night alone in his cab, periodically shoveling out his immediate environment, and listening to the radio, hoping that the DPW would send along the powerful Oshkosh four-wheel drive truck to give him a tow.

Nearby, a young woman, Linda Marston, was worried. She was trapped at home on the "main drag" – State Route 140 -- and expecting her second child to arrive around Feb. 8: then the mild contractions started. Her call to the town dispatcher asking about whether she could get plowed out because of her "situation" was met with a bemused chuckle. If necessary, she was told, maybe they could get a paramedic or doctor to her by snowmobile. Fortunately, her child waited a whole additional week, arriving on Feb. 15!

According to news reports on the 25th anniversary of the storm, Milford Fire Chief John Taddei was one of the many "first responders" who worked the storm almost continuously. In addition to his specific duties as chief, Taddei spent the better part of five days ferrying supplies to residents in need via snowmobile. The vehicle also helped provide emergency medical help and transported drivers stranded on Route 16 or Route 140 to one of the many emergency shelters set up in town.

And "routine" calls that would have been completed in minutes now took hours of time and the cooperation of far more people, the chief recalled. In one instance, the department's four-wheel drive brush fire truck was pressed into service to rush a woman in labor to the hospital.

3 TRAGEDIES ON SEA AND SHORE

Coastal communities, particularly Gloucester, Lynn, and Revere on the North Shore and Plymouth, Marshfield, Scituate and Hull on the South Shore bore the brunt of the physical damage inflicted by the storm – and the bulk of the casualties.

All told 17,000 people ended up in shelter and 10,000 were evacuated from the most dangerous areas. That was when they could be evacuated. It was a close call for many...One family in Hull had to evacuate a blind and deaf elder through deep, cold snow, water, and ice – a daunting task. In the hardest hit areas of Scituate some simply could not escape. In some cases, raging waters tore children from the grasp of parents.

Spectacularly, the *Peter Stuyvesant*, a retired former Hudson River steamboat added as a function facility at the famous Pier Four Restaurant by owner Anthony Athanas, broke free of its moorings, took on water, and sank. in Rockport, the landmark Motif #1 – a weather-beaten red shack alongside the harbor, was swept to oblivion. Another seaside landmark that fell victim to the storm was a modest dwelling in Truro made famous in The Outermost House, by author and naturalist Henry Beston. The storm turned it to matchwood.

On Boston's North Shore, with its active maritime community, the storm's progress was closely watched. Among those paying attention were the captain and crew of the Gloucester-based pilot boat, *Can Do.*

As the storm built in intensity, Capt. Frank Quirk heard with concern of the peril facing the Greek tanker *Global Hope*, which was having problems navigating through storm-tossed Salem Sound. A small Coast Guard vessel heading for the scene was also in trouble. Despite the odds, Quirk gathered his crew and headed straight for the danger. The dramatic hours that followed are described in author Michael J. Tougias's book "Ten Hours Until Dawn: The True Story of Heroism and Tragedy Aboard the Can Do," based in part on the radio transmissions of that day. In the end, the tanker and the Coast Guard vessel survived but the *Can Do*, and its whole crew, Quirk, Charlie Bucko, Norman Curley, Kenneth Fuller Jr. and Donald Wilkinson, were lost.

Bodies of her crew washed ashore over the following days. Later, the *Can*

Do was discovered, salvaged, renamed and put back in service around the North Shore.

4 RESPONSE AND RECOVERY

In addition to widespread deployment of the National Guard by both Massachusetts and Rhode Island, additional help came from the active duty Army with hundreds of soldiers flown from Fort Bragg, N.C. via dozens of airlift flights on C-130 and C-141 transports. But even getting the soldiers into the region took heroic efforts on the part of snow removal crews at Logan in Boston and at Hanscom Field in Bedford. In Massachusetts, authorities specifically tasked the Army and National Guard with the tasks of clearing the major blocked roadways such as Route 128 – and superintending removal of abandoned vehicles.

Most of the equipment needed came from private contractors within the state. According to the Army Corps of Engineers, most of the equipment needed to dig out from the storm came from private contracts, including small business and minority owned firms. Some 2,300 received state contracts that earned some $14.5 million in the immediate aftermath of the storm. The Corps also hired heavy equipment from New Hampshire, Vermont, and New York. Occasionally, needed equipment was simply commandeered.

In Massachusetts, the State of Emergency Executive Order issued by Governor Dukakis effectively closed most businesses and, most visibly, banned road travel deemed non-essential. Gov. Ella T. Grasso in Connecticut and Garrahy in Rhode Island made similar orders.

February 7 through 12, 1978, became temporary legal holidays – paid time off for most Massachusetts workers thanks to exhortations from the Governor. Among the exceptions were healthcare facilities and workers. Heating contractors, utility companies, pharmacies and then food stores joined the list of exemptions. But even then, vehicle traffic was sparse. The author hitched a ride with a doctor heading from the Western Suburbs to Mass. General Hospital and saw only a handful of other vehicles on the entire drive.

Of course, some ignored or evaded the ban and many "got away with it." Jack Mileski, with whom the author worked years later, was restless at home and decided to head for work – the Digital Equipment Corporation "Mill" in Maynard. He made it without incident – and discovered that company founder, Ken Olsen, has gotten there first!

Another colleague, at the time a teenager in Beverly, recalled joyriding with friends on the flimsy (and facetious) excuse that they were delivering groceries for a grandmother. Law enforcement bought the excuse or couldn't be bothered, so the joy ride continued. But some enforcement was harsh. Governor Dukakis shared the story of a man stopped along I-93 by military police. Lacking a valid reason to drive, his car was impounded on the spot and he was forced to walk home.

To deal with the need to shore up and repair structures, many of them located near the water and therefore under the purview of conservation commission regulations, the governor also issued an executive order. The order allowed the minimum amount of work necessary to "protect the endangered structure or property and abate the emergency," and allowed, in effect, the deputization of individual conservation commission members to inspect and bless work in progress.

5 COMMUNITY AND CAMARADERIE

Even where the storm was less destructive, it still made daily life a sobering experience. Innumerable families awoke to discover that their doors were completely blocked by snow, often necessitating exit through an upper story window. Supplies of almost everything ran low, from the cabinets of individual family kitchens to local stores and area warehouses. People had to suddenly learn to "make do."

Where drifts were high and deep, many people had great difficulty getting out of their homes and, therefore, couldn't begin to dig out. Some climbed out of windows, sometimes on the second floor, to clamber to a position from which the snow could be shoveled.

One town fire department (probably not the only one) solicited residents to borrow metal detectors so they could try to locate, and shovel out, fire hydrants lost in snow drifts and embankments.

One of the most amusing stories to come from the Blizzard was the adaptability of the Pisani family in Franklin which made a virtue of necessity, using the 10 foot embankments of snow as a source of building material to craft a huge "igloo" with three rooms on their front lawn. Taking full advantage of the novelty, they hosted cookouts by candlelight for their family and neighbors.

One Revere evacuee recalled the apocalyptic nighttime scenes of fire, wind and waves as he and other residents were evacuated in Army vehicle. That, and relief at being rescued helped spark at least one impromptu tryst.

R.A. Salvatore, a fantasy writers with millions of books in print, credits his start as an author to the Blizzard . When the storm hit, with nothing much to do while on break from Fitchburg State College, Salvatore discovered a set of J.R.R. Tolkien novels given to him by his sister. With no distractions, Salvatore quickly slipped into the land of The Hobbit and Lord of the Rings and found himself enraptured, so much so that he switched to a literature major when he returned to school. Eventually he tried his hand at the genre in the 1980s, and never looked back.

It was a storm to remember. The final tally makes for grim reading. Some 2,500 houses were reported destroyed or badly damaged. Hundreds of vehicles and boats met a similar fate, helping to keep insurance adjusters busy for a long time. And 54 people were killed. Indeed, in one of the most disturbing events of the blizzard, Max Fishman, a 64-year-old auxiliary police officer from of Randolph, was shot in the head at point-blank range and left to die in the snow on Wyoming Street in Roxbury – in effect, executed -- as he was making an emergency fuel delivery to area residents on Feb. 10, 1978. Two individuals, 15-year old Gerald Hill and 20-year-old Hubert Smith, Jr. were later convicted of the crime.

But, despite such painful incidents, for most survivors, recollections of a shared adventure and the kindnesses of strangers are a dominant memory of the Blizzard of `78.

6 THE COLOR OF A BLIZZARD

MARLBORO, MASS.:A major storm on Jan. 20, 1978 buried the area, including this street in Marlboro, Mass. under two feet of snow. (courtesy of Ric Werme)

MARLBORO, MASS.: Windows and doors buried...(courtesy of Ric Werme)

MARLBORO, MASS: View from the second story with fence posts out of sight. (courtesy of Ric Werme)

MARLBORO, MASS.: Shoulder height snow. (Ric Werme)

CAMBRIDGE, MASS.: A side street near Harvard Square. (Wayne Itano)

CAMBRIDGE, MASS.: Looking north, probably from Prescott St. toward William James Hall. (Wayne Itano)

BOSTON, MASS.: Fenway area. (courtesy of Eric Pence)

BOSTON, MASS.: A Fenway street. (courtesy of Eric Pence)

BOSTON, MASS.: Fenway area. (courtesy of Eric Pence)

BOSTON, MASS.: Find the taxi! Another Fenway area view. (courtesy of
Eric Pence)

BOSTON, MASS.: Going nowhere fast in the Fenway area.(courtesy of Eric Pence)

BOSTON, MASS.: Walking on hood-deep snow. (courtesy of Eric Pence)

BOSTON, MASS.: Rediscovering the streets. (courtesy of Eric Pence)

BOSTON, MASS.: Looking down the Charles; the Longfellow Bridge with
Cambridge to the left. (courtesy of Eric Pence)

BOSTON, MASS.: Gov. Mike Dukakis being briefed by staff. Dukakis gave credit to his team for the success of response to the storm.(DCR archive)

BOSTON, MASS.: Gov. Mike Dukakis confers with Lt. Gov. Thomas P. O'Neill Jr. (DCR archive)

BOSTON, MASS.: Gov. Mike Dukakis briefs the press and public from his storm headquarters. (DCR archive)

MARLBORO, MASS: Digging out a Mustang fastback is slow going...(courtesy of Ric Werme)

MARLBORO, MASS: Just getting a path to the street required a major effort. (courtesy of Ric Werme)

MARLBORO, MASS: Snowpocalypse. (courtesy of Ric Werme)

MARLBORO, MASS.: A street that is wide enough for at least one car.
(courtesy of Ric Werme)

MARLBORO, MASS.: Snow blowers were dwarfed by the drifts. (courtesy
or Ric Werme)

MARLBORO, MASS.: Taking a break, Blizzard of `78 style. (courtesy of Ric Werme)

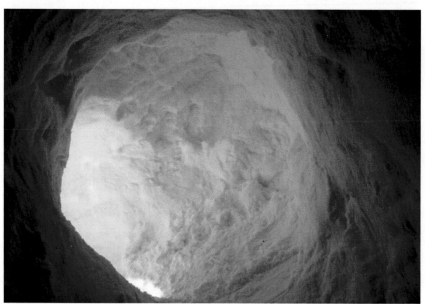

MARLBORO, MASS.: For intrepid snow fans, the depth of snow made tunneling and building a temptation that few could resist. (courtesy of Ric Werme)

BOSTON, MASS.: Park Drive impassable! (courtesy of Eric Pence)

BOSTON, MASS.: Looking across the MIT Bridge toward Cambridge with jack-knifed semitrailer. (courtesy of Eric Pence)

BOSTON, MASS.: A barely passable sidewalk. (Courtesy Eric Pence)

BOSTON, MASS.: Sunset over the Charles. Note the two figures taking a big risk and walking across the river! (Courtesy Eric Pence)

MARLBORO, MASS.: This is the early phases of recovering vehicles from I-495. (courtesy of Ric Werme)

MARLBORO, MASS.: A car buried in snow drift. (courtesy of Ric Werme)

MARLBORO, MASS.: Near Digital Equipment Corporation – a "western" scene. (courtesy of Ric Werme)

MARLBORO, MASS.: Horses often proved invaluable in the days after the storm. (courtesy of Ric Werme)

MARLBORO, MASS.: High Tech (Digital building) and high snow.
(courtesy of Ric Werme)

MARLBORO, MASS.: Workers pitch in to try to gain access to their
offices. (courtesy of Ric Werme)

MARLBORO, MASS.: Ice Station Zebra? (courtesy of Ric Werme)

CAMBRIDGE, MASS.: Central Square
looking toward Boston. (courtesy of Eric Pence)

BOSTON, MASS.: Probably Brookline Ave. (courtesy of Eric Pence)

MARLBORO, MASS.: I-495 (courtesy of Ric Werme)

MARLBORO, MASS.: Clearing the interstate. (courtesy of Ric Werme)

MARLBORO, MASS.:...and trying to avoid buried cars... (courtesy of Ric Werme)

MARLBORO, MASS.: Teamwork, and lots of it... (courtesy of Ric Werme)

EASTON, MASS.: A well-coated house (courtesy of Jonathan L. Rolfe)

EASTON, MASS.: Standing on a car to dig it out... (courtesy of Jonathan L. Rolfe)

EASTON, MASS.: Deep digging. (courtesy of Jonathan L. Rolfe)

EASTON, MASS.: Time for a brief rest. (courtesy of Jonathan L. Rolfe)

EASTON, MASS.: A skier chats with shovelers. (courtesy of Jonathan L. Rolfe)

EASTON, MASS.: Walkers make the most of traffic-free Route 138 (courtesy of Jonathan L. Rolfe)

EASTON, MASS.: Snowmobiles rule! (courtesy of Jonathan L. Rolfe)

EASTON, MASS.: Snowmobiles everywhere!
(courtesy of Jonathan L. Rolfe)

EASTON, MASS.: A pair on a grocery delivery
mission at right. (courtesy of Jonathan L. Rolfe)

EASTON, MASS.: A super highway for sleds and pedestrians. (courtesy of Jonathan L. Rolfe)

EASTON, MASS.: No traffic, and sleds used for grocery deliveries.
(courtesy of Jonathan L. Rolfe)

EASTON, MASS.: Emergencies could be problematic for patient and crew.
(courtesy of Jonathan L. Rolfe)

EASTON, MASS.: Walking in a winter wonderland.
(courtesy of Jonathan L. Rolfe)

EASTON, MASS.: Excuses? Police were checking. At least this front-wheel drive vehicle was unlikely to get stuck. (courtesy of Jonathan L. Rolfe)

EASTON, MASS.: Well, make sure you go right home and don't drive again! (courtesy of Jonathan L. Rolfe)

EVERETT, MASS.: Wellington Circle area – driving ban enforcement.
(DCR Archive)

EVERETT, MASS.: Mystic Valley Parkway near Wellington Circle. (DCR
Archive)

BOSTON, MASS.: A DPW helipad in use for emergency missions.
(DCR Archive)

CAMBRIDGE, MASS.: Skiing near Harvard Square.
(courtesy of Wayne Itano)

CAMBRIDGE, MASS.: Harvard Square, a snowy crossroad.
(courtesy of Wayne Itano)

CAMBRIDGE, MASS.: Roadway courtesies evolved quickly...(courtesy of
Wayne Itano)

CAMBRIDGE, MASS.: Après ski activities. (courtesy of Wayne Itano)

CAMBRIDGE, MASS.:There's no way to Pahk ya cah in Hahvad Yahd.
(courtesy of Wayne Itano)

CAMBRIDGE, MASS.: Snow hijinks in Harvard Yard.
(courtesy of Wayne Itano)

CAMBRIDGE, MASS.: And why not Alpine skiing (on the steps of
Widener Library? (courtesy of Wayne Itano)

CAMBRIDGE, MASS.: Or a ski jump? (courtesy of Wayne Itano)

CAMBRIDGE, MASS.: Or even a back flip? (courtesy of Wayne Itano)

NORTHSHORE, MASS.: Clearing a parkway. (DCR Archive)

SWAMPSCOTT, MASS.: Humphrey Street, Dale's Restaurant in the background, and an attempt to get rid of at least some of the snow... (DCR Archive)

BOSTON, MASS.: The sunken *Peter Stuyvesant* at Pier Four. (DCR Archive)

HULL, MASS.: Nantasket Beach damage. (DCR Archive)

HULL, MASS.: Shoreline damage. (DCR Archive)

HULL, MASS.: Shore and structure damage. (DCR Archive)

HULL, MASS.: Stabilizing shorelines, removing debris, on Feb 12. Notice both civilian and military equipment in use. (DCR Archive)

REVERE, MASS.: Frolics Ballroom ice and snow damage. (DCR Archive)

ROCKPORT, MASS.: Devastation at Pigeon Cove.
Photo by Joseph E. Pelczarski)

ROCKPORT, MASS.: Another view of Pigeon Cove area. (Photo by
Joseph E. Pelczarski)

ROCKPORT, MASS.: Storm surf reportedly topped the jetty in the background. (Photo by Joseph E. Pelczarski)

ROCKPORT, MASS.: The remains of Motif #1, the famous red storage shack in Rockport Harbor. (Photo by Joseph E. Pelczarski)

FRAMINGHAM, MASS.: Just before dawn a few days after the Blizzard. (A. Macmillan)

FRANKLIN, MASS.: A utility truck is nearly hidden from view by the snowbanks on Pond Street. (courtesy of Paul Compton)

FRANKLIN, MASS.: The Compton Sprinkler Co., nearly buried.

FRANKLIN, MASS.: Vicki Buchanio shows off her Snoopy and dog house snow creation in her Blizzard-transformed Main Street backyard. (courtesy of Vicki Buchanio)

ABOUT THE AUTHOR

Alan R. Earls is a Boston-area business and technology writer – and a local historian with a strong focus on the region's high-tech industries. At the time of the Blizzard of `78, Earls worked as a computer operator at the C.S. Draper Laboratory in Cambridge, Mass. Earls is also the founder of Via Appia Press (www.viaappiapress.com).

Made in United States
North Haven, CT
30 January 2022

15408920R00040